HOMES

Jeff Stanfield

WAYLAND

See for yourself

Homes • School • Shops • The Street • Transport

HOW TO USE THIS BOOK

This book will help you find out all about homes. All the questions highlighted in **bold** have answers on pages 26–27, but try to work them out for yourself, first. Investigate the homes near you by trying some of the detective activities on pages 28–29. You'll find difficult words explained on page 30.

All the photographs in this book were taken in Brighton. So you can compare the homes in Brighton to the homes near you.

Editor: Polly Goodman
Book designer: Jean Wheeler
Cover designer: Dome Design

First published in 1997 by Wayland Publishers Ltd
61 Western Road, Hove, East Sussex BN3 1JD, England

British Library Cataloguing in Publication Data
Stanfield, Jeff
Homes. – (See For Yourself)
1. Dwellings – England – Brighton – Juvenile literature
I. Title
307.3'36'0942256

ISBN 0 7502 1886 X

Typeset by Jean Wheeler, England
Printed and bound in Italy by G. Canale & C.S.p.A., Turin

CONTENTS

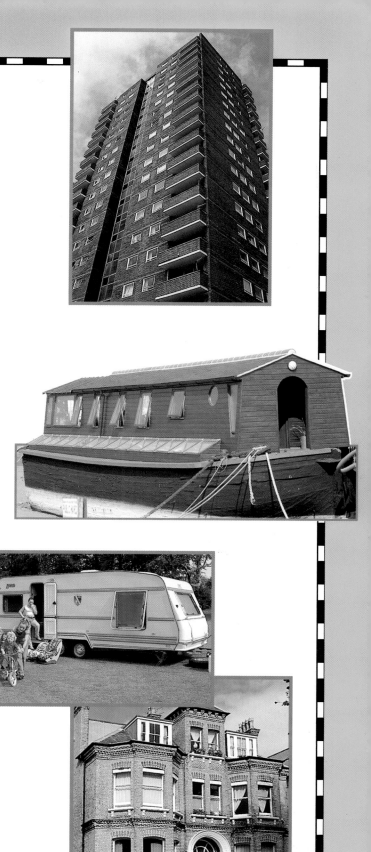

BUILDING HOMES

New homes are built using different materials and tools.

This house is half built. ▶
Can you see the grey breeze-blocks and red bricks that have been used to build the walls? Scaffolding has been put up.

Do you know what scaffolding does?

◀ This builder is mixing cement in a cement mixer.

What will the cement be used for?

This bricklayer is building a wall  using bricks, cement and a trowel. The trowel is specially shaped to spread the cement between the bricks.

▲ This roof is half built. A wooden frame is built first. Many of the sloping roofs you see every day have wooden frames.

Finally, tiles are nailed into place by  a tiler.

Why do you think the tiles overlap each other?

WINDOWS AND DOORS

Windows and doors are different shapes and sizes.

◀ This is a large, bay window.

This is a smaller, ▶ casement window.

Which window gives more space inside the house?

What type of windows do you have in your home?

These front doors belong ▶
to two different homes.
The homes are separated
by a wall inside.

Can you see the spyhole in
the blue door?

Do you know what it is for?

◀ This door is shared by
many different homes.

Each home has its own
doorbell by the side
of the door.

The girl is pressing the doorbell
of her friend's home.

Her friend can open the door
by pressing a button inside.

ROOFS

Not all roofs look the same.

Some are different shapes, or made using different materials.

These are roofs of ▶ new houses. They are covered with tiles.

◀ These older roofs are different from the new roofs.

They have chimneys and chimney pots.

Do you know why there are chimneys on the older roofs?

Underneath the roof is the attic.

These roofs ▶ have windows in their attics.

Not all attics have windows.

Are there any houses with attic windows near you?

Not all roofs are sloping.

◀ This house has a flat roof.

Why do you think sloping roofs work well in places with lots of rain?

TYPES OF HOUSES

◀ These are semi-detached houses. They are always joined together in pairs.

This is a terraced house. ▶ It was built over 100 years ago in Victorian times.

Terraced houses are joined together in rows.

How is the terraced house different from the semi-detached houses?

◀ Detached houses stand on their own.

They are not joined to other houses.

They usually have a garage and more space around them.

Some people live in ▶ bungalows. Unlike other houses, all the rooms in a bungalow are on the ground.

Older people often live in bungalows.

Why do you think this is?

Do you or your friends live in houses like these?

FLATS

A flat is a home where all the rooms are on one level. There are flats in different types of buildings.

▼ These are blocks of flats. They have four different levels.

▲ Here is a high-rise block.

How many levels can you see?

How are the two blocks of flats on this page similar and different?

Sometimes flats are built for special groups of people.

These are sheltered flats ▶ for older people. A warden also lives here to help them.

◀ This house used to be one home. Now it is divided into six flats.

▼ You can tell there are flats inside because there is an entryphone in the doorway like this one.

Do you know how to use an entryphone?

HOUSING AREAS

Many high-rise blocks ▶
like these were built
about thirty years ago
to save space.

**Why do high-rise blocks
save more space in towns
and cities?**

◀ This is an older area
of terraced houses.

The terraces are in long
rows which are close
together.

These areas tend to
have long, straight
roads.

▲ This is a newer housing area, called an estate.

The roads are much shorter than the ones in the older terraced area. They are closed at one end.

▲ How are the houses in the estate different from the terraced houses?

15

CARING FOR HOMES

The weather wears buildings away so homes need to be looked after.

 This lady is painting a wooden door.

Why is it important to paint woodwork?

Gardens and yards need caring for, otherwise they can become overgrown.

This girl is weeding the border. ▶

What other jobs might have to be done in the garden or yard during the year?

16

Sometimes houses need really big repairs.

▼ This man is working on a flat roof. He is covering it with a waterproof material.

What would happen if the roof was not covered?

Homes needing big repairs usually have scaffolding up around them. Are there any buildings with scaffolding near you?

CHANGING HOMES

People sometimes change
their homes.

This man is screwing in new, ▶
double-glazed windows.
These are two layers of glass
with air in between.

**Why might people have double
glazing put in?**

◀ This is a new wall being
built inside a house. The wall
will divide the room into two.

The wooden framework has been
built. Soon, wallboards will be
nailed to it.

◀ This man is building an attic room.

▼ This is the house from the outside.
It is a very big job.

Why might people want a room in their attic?

Sometimes people change homes completely by moving house.

◀ They need to hire a removal lorry to move all their furniture.

MOBILE HOMES

People do not always live
in houses.

This family lives in a caravan. ▶
It can be towed from place to
place. Caravans are a type of
mobile home.

◀ These homes belong to a group of
New Age travellers.

They like moving around
the countryside.

All the travellers'
belongings must be
carried in their vehicles.

◀ **What belongings can
you see in this picture?**

If you could move your home to another place, where would you move it to?

What would you take with you?

▲ House boats are a different type of mobile home. This one is moored near the sea.

Where else could you live on a boat like this?

This is inside a house boat. ▶ How are the windows different from the ones in your home?

HOLIDAY HOMES

People can stay in lots of different types
of homes when they go on holiday.

◄ **What type of
holiday home is
the Rockhaven?**

Look at the blue
writing in the window.

This backpackers' hotel is above
a pasta resturant. ▶

What groups of people is it for?

◀ This hotel is very big and modern.

It costs much more to stay here than in the backpackers' hotel.

How can you tell that this is a very modern hotel?

These people like staying ▶ in a tent on holiday.

They can carry their tent with them and stay where they like.

What is your favourite type of holiday home?

HOMELESSNESS

Many people do not have homes.

Homeless people can be young or old.

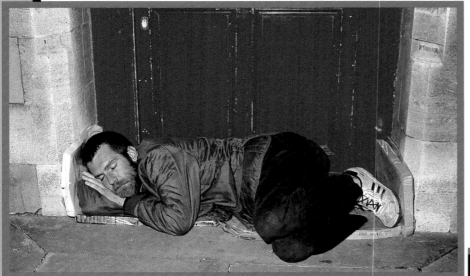

◀ This homeless person is sleeping rough. He is using cardboard to sleep on for warmth.

Can you see where he is sleeping?

Soup kitchens ▶ like this one help to feed homeless people.

This young person has managed to find a room in a hostel for the homeless.

Why might this be better than sleeping rough on the street?

It takes a lot of money to help care for the homeless.

This lady is selling ▶ a special magazine that raises money for homeless people.

It is called *The Big Issue*.

ANSWERS TO QUESTIONS

Pages 4–5
Building Homes

Scaffolding helps builders reach the higher floors of buildings.

The cement will be spread between the bricks and the breeze-blocks to hold them together.

Tiles overlap each other so that rain does not get in between them.

Pages 6–7 Windows and Doors

The bay window gives more space inside the house because of its shape.

The spyhole lets the person inside see who is at the door before they open it.

Pages 8–9 Roofs

There are chimneys on the older roofs because they were built when coal fires were the only type of heating. The newer houses have gas or electric heating, which do not need a chimney because there is no smoke.

Rainwater runs off sloping roofs more easily than flat roofs.

Pages 10–11 Types of Houses

The terraced house is joined on both sides and has no room for a garage.

Older people often live in bungalows so that they do not have to climb any stairs.

Pages 12–13
Flats

There are seventeen levels in the high-rise block shown in the photo. But there are more levels below that the photo does not show.

Both blocks have lots of balconies and flat roofs. The high-rise block is higher than the low-rise block.

To use an entryphone, first push the button of the flat you are visiting. When you hear the person inside, speak to them through the entryphone. They can open the front door to let you in by pushing a button inside.

Pages 14–15 Housing Areas

High-rise blocks save space because they contain many homes on a small area of land.

The houses in the estate are all detached, with garages and large gardens.

Pages 16–17 Caring for Homes

It is important to paint woodwork to protect it from drying out in the sun and rotting in the rain.

Other jobs are mowing the lawn, sweeping leaves and trimming hedges.

If the roof was not covered, rainwater would get inside the building and make it damp.

Pages 18–19 Changing Homes

Double glazing helps keep houses warm. It also stops sound, like traffic and aeroplane noise, coming in from outside.

Attic rooms give homes more space. They create an extra room.

Pages 20–21 Mobile Homes

There is a spade, a coffee pot, a kettle, a gas bottle and rugs near the fire. There is a cooker and clothes in the back of the green van.

You could live on a house boat on a river, canal or lake.

Pages 22–23 Holiday Homes

The Rockhaven is a bed-and-breakfast hotel. Guests pay for a room, and breakfast in the morning.

The backpackers' hotel is a cheap hotel for backpackers, students or tourists with little money.

You can tell it is a very modern hotel because it has been built using lots of glass.

Pages 24–25 Homelessness

The man is sleeping in a doorway.

A hostel is better than the street for homeless people because it has a bed, a place to wash and hot food.

DETECTIVE ACTIVITIES

It's great fun investigating homes. Why not become a homes detective and try some of the activities below.

● Find a building site. Watch the work going on through the safety fences. BUILDING SITES ARE DANGEROUS PLACES SO DO NOT GO IN. Make a list of the jobs, materials and any tools you can see. Do you know what each tool is used for?

● How many different types of windows can you see near your home?

● Make a matching game. Draw pictures of five doors in a street near you. Then draw pictures of the houses they belong to. Can your friends match the doors to the houses?

● Make a model to show your friends that rainwater runs off sloping roofs, but often stays on flat roofs. Is it true that the steeper the roof, the faster the water runs off?

● Snap! Cut out pictures of different types of homes from your local paper. Cut out terraced, detached and semi-detached houses, flats, caravans and bungalows. Stick them on to plain post cards. When you have got enough, you can play houses snap with a friend.

28

● Draw a picture of your favourite house. Label all the parts of the house. Draw a picture map of the way to the house from your home. If it is your home, draw a picture plan of it.

● Hold a competition between friends to see who can find the tallest block of flats near your home. Count the number of floors in each block.

● Keep a home-watch diary. Every weekend, write lists of the jobs you see people doing on their homes. Look for jobs like painting or gardening.

● If you have a garden, draw a plan of it, or draw a plan of your local park. Use labels to show where different jobs have to be done, like mowing the lawn and weeding the borders.

● Look in your local library for books with old pictures of your local area. How have the houses changed since these pictures were taken?

● Look at an old map of your area in the library. Can you see any places where new homes have been built since the map was made?

● Ask older members of your family, like your grandparents, what homes used to have in them when they were your age. How have things changed?

● Find the oldest and newest houses near your home. Draw a picture of each of them. Write down a list of how they are different.

DIFFICULT WORDS

Backpackers Tourists or travellers who carry their luggage in a rucksack.

Bay window Usually a curved window that comes out from the wall.

Breeze-block Building blocks made from cement and cinders.

Bungalow A house with only one floor.

Casement window A window with hinges on one side so it opens outwards.

Detached house A single house that is not joined to others.

Double glazing Windows that have two panes of glass, which help to keep homes warmer and quieter.

Entryphone A type of doorbell system. It allows people in flats to talk to people at the front door and let them in by pressing a button.

Estate An area of land designed to have buildings on it.

Extensions Extra parts of a house that are added on to make it bigger.

Housing estate An area of land with modern houses planned and built on it.

Hostel A place where people can stay, often for short periods of time.

Mobile Easily moved.

Moored Attached to a fixed object. Houseboats are moored by ropes to riverbanks or quays to stop them moving.

Scaffolding A framework of metal tubes and wooden planks, which helps builders reach high spots when they are building or repairing homes.

Trowel A small tool with a flat, pointed blade.

Victorian The time when Queen Victoria ruled Britain, from 1837–1901.

Warden A person who looks after others, or keeps watch over them.

Other Books to Read

History from Objects at Home by Karen Bryant-Mole (Wayland, 1993)

Houses and Homes by Paul Humphries (Evans, 1994)

Houses Around the World by Godfrey Hall (Wayland, 1995)

Landmarks: Exploring Inner Cities by A. Earl & D. Sensier (Wayland, 1997)

Landmarks: Exploring Seaside Towns by A. Earl & D. Sensier (Wayland, 1997)

Landmarks: Exploring Suburbs by Jonathon Baldwin (Wayland, 1997)

Landmarks: Exploring Villages by A. Earl & D. Sensier (Wayland, 1997)

Starting Geography: Houses and Homes by Helen Barden (Wayland, 1992)

Take Care At Home by Carole Wale (Wayland, 1996)

Technology Topics: Houses and Homes by Chris Oxlade (Watts, 1994)

Timelines: Houses by Fiona Macdonald (Watts, 1993)

Topic Box: Houses and Homes by Rhoda Nottridge (Wayland, 1996)

You can find out more about homes in your area by visiting a local library or museum and looking at maps and photographs.

INDEX

Page numbers in **bold** show that there is a photograph aswell as information.